There Is No Misery Where There Is No Want

LIFE LESSONS FROM INDIA'S SPIRITUAL MASTERS

ALEPH

ALEPH BOOK COMPANY
An independent publishing firm
promoted by *Rupa Publications India*

First published in India in 2023
by Aleph Book Company
7/16 Ansari Road, Daryaganj
New Delhi 110 002

ISBN: 978-93-95853-79-8

1 3 5 7 9 10 8 6 4 2

Printed in India

CONTENTS

INTRODUCTION

Life is uncertain. All of us have to deal with fear, desire, loss, and bad luck. But are pain and grief unavoidable? Can we overcome suffering? How can we achieve happiness? What does being successful mean to each of us? Can we be content with worldly success and material gains? Or do we need to focus on fulfilment and growth of our inner lives?

Questions such as these have been pondered upon by both philosophers and common people throughout the ages. India has been home to many of these saints and sages. From Mahavira and the Buddha who lived over 2,000 years ago, to philosophers of the nineteenth and twentieth centuries, like Sri Ramakrishna and Swami Vivekananda, they have inspired millions who follow their teachings and have found solace in their lessons.

Culled from the essential teachings of these great Indian masters, the lessons in this volume will help the reader understand their place in the world, define their relationship with others in the community, and find ways to approach the spiritual. While most of these philosophers examine spiritual wisdom, their insights are not only for ascetics or renunciates. Householders, professionals, parents, students—everyone—can find ways to adapt these lessons in their daily lives and find a life of contentment. These can lead to a deeper understanding of life's mysteries, offer pathways to knowledge and understanding, and reveal the true meaning of success and happiness.

This volume collects insights and wisdom from some of the world's greatest teachers including Swami Vivekananda, Adi Shankara, Lal Ded, and Hazrat Nizamuddin.

.1.

WHO AM I?

Man can know God only when he knows himself. 'Who am I?'—when you try to reflect on this carefully, you'll see that there is in fact nothing called 'I'. Hands, feet, blood, flesh, and so on—which one of these is 'I'? When you peel an onion layer after layer, you will only get the skin, and no substance. Similarly, when you reason, you will see that there is no 'I'! What remains is the atman—consciousness. When the 'I'-ness of the 'I' disappears, God appears before us.

—Sri Ramakrishna

If you know that the Self is precious,
protect it, guard it.

A learned person should keep awake.
First, one should settle his own self in what is proper;
then, he should instruct others.
Thus a learned person will not suffer.

If one wants to make oneself what one instructs
others to be,
one should discipline oneself with great restraint.
Indeed, one's self is difficult to discipline.
One who irrigates the fields, verily, leads the water
where he wants;
an arrow-maker bends the arrow; a carpenter bends
the timber; a man of pious life controls his Self.

—The Buddha

Pure consciousness was such bliss,
all veils of illusion and thought lifted.
Spontaneously I realized my whole Self.
And Lal bloomed like a lotus in the mud.

Rituals and fasting are not the real way
nor the adoption of special attire.
Fulfilling bodily desires is not it either.
Contemplate the true Self; this is the best advice!

—Lal Ded

The Self is known to every one of us,
man, woman or child,
and even to animals.
Without knowing Him
we can neither live nor move,
nor have our being;
without knowing this Lord of all, we cannot
breathe or live a second.

—Swami Vivekananda

When ignorance is destroyed,
the soul shines by itself,
as does the sun when a cloud passes.
Knowledge purifies the ignorance-stained
Self and disappears
as soap-nut-tree powder does in water.

Give up desire, anger, greed and delusion,
and ask yourself, 'Who am I?'

True knowledge is comprehension that the Self is
true and everything else is false.

Not having a mind, I have
no desire, grief, hatred or fear.
Indeed, the scriptures declare
that the Self has no mind.
It is pure.

—**Adi Shankara**

.2.

ATTACHMENT

Why did I let myself sink in a sea of attachments?
Slush and mire now abound. The shore is
long lost sight of.
In the end we will all die.
Who will release us from the fear of death?

I have not known wealth since birth
nor luxuries and greed for them.
Content with little food, poverty, and hardship,
all I have known is love for God.

Whether the world venerates me or shuns me
I alone will bear the consequences
of my detached actions,
which are offered to my own Self.
So wherever I go, I will prosper!

—Lal Ded

It is because we mistakenly see ourselves
as separate from everything else
that we become attached.
If we fully appreciate that nothing is really
separate to begin with,
attachment becomes impossible.

He is the knower of the path of love (of God) who
relinquishes attachment to both the worlds.

—Moinuddin Chishti

Life is as unstable as water on a lotus leaf.
Yet the whole world is devoured by
conceit and sorrow.

When youth is gone, what is the use of lust?
When water has evaporated, what is
the use of the lake?
When money has gone, where are one's relatives?
When Truth is known, where is the worldly bond?

—Adi Shankara

Ignorant people who earn money
through evil actions
earn the resentment of others.
They leave all their wealth behind
and go to hell.
A violent person does not understand
that life is perishable.
Being attached to worldly objects,
he dares to commit sin.
He toils day and night, assuming his body
to be imperishable.
He tries to earn more and more wealth.

—**Mahavira**

One's faith is incomplete
until all worldly desires
and attachments mean the same
as a piece of stone.

—**Hazrat Nizamuddin**

Work is not the goal of life; it is just
the beginning of the story.
Work without attachment is a path for
God-realization, not the goal.

Worldly people get bound in this world because
of their desires; their hands and feet get tied. And
they think that all happiness lies in this pursuit of
worldly pleasure.... They don't know that it is this
very thing that brings upon death. When worldly
people die, their wives weep, saying 'You left us
like this! What will happen to me!' But so great is
their worldly attachment that the very next moment,
when they see the lamp burning too bright, they
say, 'Lower the wick, it's using too much oil.' While
death is standing just round the corner!

—Sri Ramakrishna

.3.

DESIRE

One who knows the Self has attained
Brahman, having crossed world
lines in this life itself.
The Vedas say that one who knows the
Self transcends sorrow.
The Smritis say that one who attains
knowledge of the Supreme Being
does not care where his body falls,
since he has destroyed all desires.

When the body is old and the hair is grey,
when he is toothless and has to walk
with the help of a stick,
the old man still does not lose desire.

Dedicate all your actions to the Lord.
Renounce all desire for the pleasures of material
objects, which are riddled with pain.
Seek the Supreme Being constantly.

—Adi Shankara

Self-mortification is useless if the
Self lusts after pleasures.
He who has extinguished the Self is free from lust.
He desires no pleasures, the satisfaction of
his natural wants will not defile him.
He may eat and drink according to
his body's needs.

The sensual man is a slave to his desires,
but seeking pleasures is disgusting.

A word spoken in anger is the sharpest sword,
desire is the deadliest poison,
lust is the fiercest fire,
ignorance is the darkest night.

Those who are enlightened and in full control of
their minds and are no longer clinging to earthly
pleasures, they have reached Nirvana.

—The Buddha

The dreadful tree of desires brings
forth dreadful fruits;
if this tree is permanently uprooted,
you can live peacefully.

He who is rid of delusion
destroys his sorrow;
he who is rid of desire
destroys his delusion;
he who is rid of greed
destroys his desire;
he who owns nothing
destroys his greed.

A little water can extinguish fire.
But the waters of all the oceans
will not be enough to
extinguish the fires of
desire and delusion.

The mind of man is fickle.
He wants to fulfil all his desires, which is
as likely as filling a sieve with water.

—**Mahavira**

If you feed your desires, they grow.
Starve them and they diminish.
Eliminate them and you receive everything.

Do nothing for the sake of any desire.
Seek no pleasure or satisfaction
from your actions.
Be a man of God—
every intention of yours
should be for the sake of God.

Denounce the desires
that cage you and free yourself,
see how a thousand favourites
sit before you.

—Hazrat Nizamuddin

Rid yourself of desires for material objects
and focus on the true Self.
It is not hard to access, and is near you.
Search not far. Just pay attention to It.

—Lal Ded

What is a mind free from desire like? It is like a dry matchstick—you rub it once and it will catch fire immediately. But when you try to light a wet match, you may rub it again and again till it breaks, but it will not burn. Similarly, when you give spiritual instruction to a simple, truthful, and pure-minded person, he immediately develops love for God. On the other hand, no matter how many times you instruct worldly people, it is to no avail.

—Sri Ramakrishna

Religion comes with intense self-sacrifice.
Desire nothing for yourself.
Do all for others.
This is to live and move and
have your being in God.

There is no misery
where there is no want.
Desire, want, is the father of all misery.
Desires are bound
by the laws of success
and failure.

—Swami Vivekananda

.4.

PAIN AND SUFFERING

Do not hurt he who is the cause of your suffering.
Never hurt or harm living creatures.
One who has no sympathy for any living
thing is an outcast.

If a person does evil, let him not repeat it.
Accumulation of evil is suffering.

Birth is suffering;
old age is suffering;
disease is suffering;
death is suffering;
sorrow and misery are suffering;
affliction and despair are suffering.
The loss of that which we love
and cannot attain is suffering.

The cause of pain is to be abandoned,
the cessation of pain is to be realized,
the noble Eightfold Path is to be practised.

—The Buddha

Deep suffering is calamitous like a lightning strike
and painful like being crushed in a flour mill.
It is despair like darkness at noon.
But suffer well, for suffering will lighten the
burden that is your ego.

—Lal Ded

If you cannot tolerate pain
from the words and deeds of others,
do you have the right to cause pain
to others through your words and deeds?

All beings wander and suffer
according to their previously acquired karmas.
Without experiencing the fruit of their karmas,
they will never be liberated.

Non-violence and kindness towards living
beings is kindness to yourself.
For you are saved from sinning and
the consequent suffering.
Thus you can ensure your happiness.

—Mahavira

Patience is tested through resignation to sorrow,
sufferings, and disaster
without murmur or disclosing one's pains to others.

—Moinuddin Chishti

We must take into consideration
the great objection against work: that it causes pain.
All misery and pain come from attachment.
It is ninety to one that the human being
whom I have helped
will prove ungrateful and go against me;
and the result to me is pain.
Such things deter mankind
from working.

May I be born again and again
and suffer thousands of miseries,
so that I may worship
the only God that exists—
the only God I believe in,
the sum total of all souls, my God of the wicked,
my God of the miserable,
my God of the poor
of all races, of all species.

—Swami Vivekananda

.5.

ILLUSION

I know not from where I have come and how.
Nor where and how I will go hereafter.
What wealth will serve me on this journey?
How does one trust this precarious breath?

—Lal Ded

He understands that rebirth is destroyed,
the religious life has been led,
done is what was to be done,
there is nought for him beyond this world.

—The Buddha

The duality which is called the world
is mere illusion.
Non-duality is the supreme truth.
Hence no world either as evolving or
dissolving exists.

When knowledge arises, like the light of the sun,
illusion or maya is removed.
There is the realization that the Supreme Being is
without beginning or end...
without birth or death or decay, and is fearless.

—Adi Shankara

They that cross the expanse of ocean,
making a bridge across the pools,
while the people bind rafts—
they that have reached the other shore are the wise.
The learned noble disciple feels
loathing for the body;
feeling disgust he becomes free from passion;
through freedom from passion he is emancipated.

Everyone knows of the acute suffering
of birth, old age and death;
but nobody develops detachment
from sensual pleasures.
How severe is the knot of illusion?

We believe wrongly that
someone else controls our destiny and
makes us happy or unhappy.
We alone, not some imaginary supreme power,
are responsible for our destinies.

We create our own misfortune
and become entangled in it;
we remain trapped within the painful
cycle of birth, death, and rebirth.

—Mahavira

It is enough to have faith in one path. If you
believe in formless God, that is good. However, do
not think that this alone is true and all else is false.
Know that formless God is true and God with
form is also true.

—Sri Ramakrishna

This mixture of life and death,
good and evil,
knowledge and ignorance
is called maya—the universal phenomenon.
You may go on for eternity
seeking happiness.
You find much,
and much evil too.
To have good and no evil
is childish nonsense.

—Swami Vivekananda

With devotion and worship we come closer
to experiencing God's generosity.
It is at this stage that we need a guide.
He will break our illusions of perfection
and teach us the impermanence of reason.
His guidance will liberate you
and reveal the truth to you.

—Hazrat Nizamuddin

.6.

CONQUER THE SELF

There is no enemy outside your soul.
The real enemies live
inside you—anger, pride, greed,
attachment, and hatred.

Just as a tortoise withdraws into its own shell,
a wise man should withdraw himself from evil
by spiritual exertion.

Pride, which is like a pillar of stone,
prevents a person from being humble
and drags the soul to hell.
One who humiliates others
out of pride is ignorant.

—Mahavira

Like a bow made of wood that won't bend
and arrows of hollow reed,
like a badly built house,
or a shop without a vendor,
life without consciousness is futile.

Recognize and anticipate lust, anger, and greed,
and destroy them
with good thoughts and self-control.
Or they will destroy you!

—Lal Ded

Do not ask for anything,
take what is given to you.
Keep what you need,
give the rest away to someone who needs it.

A sincere atonement of a sin
and having committed none at all
are equal in the eyes of God.

In arguments and conversations there should
be no place for anger, pride,
and arrogance even if you are among friends.

—Hazrat Nizamuddin

There are ten bad things, and by avoiding
them you become good.
They are the three evils of the body, four evils of
the tongue, and three evils of the mind.
The three evils of the body are murder,
theft, and adultery.
The four evils of the tongue are lying,
slander, abuse, and idle talk.
The three evils of the mind are covetousness,
hatred, and error.

—The Buddha

Give up your insatiable desire for wealth,
be satisfied with what you have,
the fruits of your own labour.

—Adi Shankara

If one whose heart is not pure
and faith is not strong
indulges in money-making,
he is harming society and committing a major sin.

—Moinuddin Chishti

Vedanta recognizes no sin.
If there is sin, this is the only sin—
to say that you are weak,
or others are weak.

—Swami Vivekananda

.7.

PEACE

Atman or the Self is the nature of the Supreme Being,
a state of knowledge and absolute bliss.

He whose mind is united with the Supreme Being
and is at great peace is
not merely a knower of Brahman
but is Brahman itself.
Such a person, whoever he may be, is fit to be
worshipped by the gods.
O Lord, in the form of this body,
I am your servant.
In the form of life, I am a part of you.
In the form of soul, you are within me and in every
other being or animal that I behold.

—Adi Shankara

The more you advance towards God, the greater
peace you experience. Peace, peace, peace, great
peace. The nearer you get to the Ganges,
the cooler you feel. Take a dip and you will feel
even more peaceful.

—**Sri Ramakrishna**

When other cravings ceased, peace came to me.
I prepared my heart in the pestle of love.
Then emblazoned it and partook of it.
Now if I live or die, it's all the same to me!

—Lal Ded

Live with love in your heart;
violence shall die its own death and
all shall live in peace.

Remember that without a pious heart, our prayer
neither reaches the Almighty
nor can we live in peace.

Overflow with peace and joy, and scatter them
wherever you are and wherever you go.
Be a blazing fire of Truth, be a beauteous blossom
of Love and a soothing balm of Peace.

—Moinuddin Chishti

.8.

FORGIVENESS

Anger begets more anger.
Forgiveness and love lead to
more forgiveness and love.

By conquering anger,
the soul attains forgiveness.

At the root of all sinful acts
is our passion for possessions.
Cultivate forgiveness
to eliminate anger,
humility to control ego,
honesty to avoid deceit and
satisfaction to be free of greed.

—Mahavira

Kindness and forgiveness are the virtues to be
practised to perfection.
When one prays it should be
for the salvation of all.
Raise your spirit to a higher level of
consciousness.

—Hazrat Nizamuddin

.9.

DEATH

Ishvara is hidden by the falsity of maya.
As long as there is a difference between jiva and
Ishvara, birth and death will not go. Therefore,
never differentiate between jiva and Ishvara.
Studying the Bhagavad Gita, drinking
the water of the Ganga,
and worshipping the Lord will save
you from fear of death.

—Adi Shankara

Happiness and sorrow, birth and death, disease and
grief—all these exist so long as one has the idea that
'I am this body'. These belong to the body, not to
atman...after one attains knowledge of the Self, one
sees happiness and suffering, and birth and
death as dream-like.

—Sri Ramakrishna

Life is short
but the soul is eternal.
One thing being certain, death,
let us take up a great ideal, and
give up the whole life to it.
May He, the Lord,
who comes again and again
for the salvation of His people,
may He bless us and
lead us all to the fulfilment of our aims.

Worship the terrible!
Worship death!
All else is vain.
All struggle is vain.
That is the last lesson.
Yet this is not the coward's love of death,
not the love of the weak,
or the suicide.
It is the welcome of the strong man,
who has sounded everything to its depths,
and knows that there is no alternative.

Strength is life; weakness is death.
Strength is felicity, life eternal, immortal.
Weakness is constant strain and misery,
weakness is death.

—Swami Vivekananda

One who harms beings that are
longing for happiness,
such a one will not secure happiness after death.
One who does not strike beings that
long for happiness,
such a one will secure happiness after death.

Death seizes a man who collects only flowers here
and there, whose mind is distracted, like a great
flood in a sleeping village.

—The Buddha

If you believe you can never be impure.
Go forward on the path of God in whatever
appearance you came in.
One with a taste of unquestionable devotion
can never feel attracted to the mundane in life.
Such a person will embrace death with sincerity.

—Hazrat Nizamuddin

Alert, when Lal entered her heart
she witnessed the union of Shiva and Shakti there!
She dissolved into an ocean of nectar.
Transcending life while still alive thus, Death had
no business with Lal anymore!

Chariots, thrones, pomp, and pleasure
are forever, you think.
Why then is the fear of death
never far from you?

Oh why did I lose myself in attachment to others!
Why did I see falsehood as truth?
Deluded, in thrall to the senses now,
one is stuck in the cycle of birth and death.

—Lal Ded

The soul wanders
through the cycle of birth and death
and is bound by eight karmas.
These eight karmas are
obstruction of knowledge, vision, feelings,
delusions, longevity, form, status,
and power.

Knowing all this, he who does not
walk the path of righteousness in this birth
as a human repents
at the time of death.

A person under delusion suffers from
the cycle of birth and death.

One who is obedient to his teacher
and is humble
crosses the ocean of birth and death
and attains liberation.

—Mahavira

Life is meant to be lived with good health,
peace, joy, and optimism.
But in all your moments of life and joy, remember
always death, the destroyer of delights.

Do not wish for death but instead pray,
'O Lord, keep me alive so long as life may be good
for me and let me die when it is time
for me so to do.'

The dervish regards death as a friend,
luxury as an enemy
and the constant remembrance of God as glory.

—**Moinuddin Chishti**

.10.

GOD THE BELOVED,
GOD THE DIVINE

The heart was essentially created for
falling in love with God and his creations.
When we transcend the external world
just as the snake sheds its skin,
we find the lover, the beloved and
love to be one.

God is love, lover, and beloved.
The dual aspect of the Divine Being,
in the form of love and beauty,
has glorified the universe and produced harmony.

—Moinuddin Chishti

Are you the one who asks the gardener to
close the gates of the garden
when you and your Beloved
(God) are inside?
Open the gates to all, let
everyone bask in
God's benediction.

It is the love of God
that is the absolute purpose
behind the creation of life.
So surrender your heart
to the Maker in complete allegiance.

—Hazrat Nizamuddin

I am not bound by merits or sins, nor by happiness
or sorrow, nor am I bound by sacred hymns or
sacred places, sacred scriptures or rituals, I am
neither enjoyment, nor an object to be enjoyed,
nor the enjoyer, I am the ever pure blissful
consciousness; I am auspicious, I am Shiva...

I am not the imaginary I, the ego, my name. I am
not the temporary I, my body or my mind. I am the
everlasting Life Force behind all living beings.
I am the source of Universal Love and Happiness.
Aham Brahmasmi—I am Brahman...
I am without attribute and actions, eternal,
immaculate and unchanging, formless,
ever free and pure.

I pervade everything inside and outside.
I am the same in all.
I am eternal, unattached, pure, and motionless.

Having seen the Supreme Being, there is nothing
else to be seen.
There is no rebirth and nothing else to be known.

Realize this in order to be the Supreme Being,
which is across, above, below, all-pervading existence,
knowledge, bliss and which is non-dual,
infinite, and eternal.

—Adi Shankara

One does not experience premabhakti unless one
has an intense love for God. And along with it the
feeling that 'God is my own'.

If you ask which form of God to contemplate
upon—meditate on any form that you like.
But know that all represent the same God...

The same Supreme Being is called 'Mother'.
Mother is the source of great love.
God can be attained through love.

—**Sri Ramakrishna**

Drunk on the ocean of worldly pursuits
many are the games I have played,
forms I have taken,
many the births and deaths endured.
Why? What is wrong with me?
When I am Shakti herself!

—Lal Ded

It is not the God in temples,
symbols, and images
that we are to worship.
It is not the God in the high heaven,
whom we cannot see,
that we are to worship.

—Swami Vivekananda

.11.

PRAYER AND RITUAL

The results of rituals, like going to heaven and so
on, do not come within one's experience.
There is reason to doubt whether they
will ever happen.
But the results of 'knowledge' lie
within human experience.

One cannot both meditate and perform rituals as
the two are mutually opposite to each other.

Since self-realization is immediate, there is
no need to fear about getting the result.

By doing rituals, whose results—like attaining
heaven—do not come in a lifetime,
there is reason to doubt whether they
will ever happen or not.

When a person achieves knowledge,
he ceases to perform rituals.

—**Adi Shankara**

Requesting favours from a supreme power
through sacrificial offerings or chanting mantras
is useless.
The power to liberate your soul
rests within you.

Do not practise austerities
for this life or another.
Do not practise austerities for praise,
status, fame, or name.
Practise austerities only to destroy karmas.

—Mahavira

I recited mantras till my palate wore thin.
I turned the prayer bead till my fingers bruised.
Yet I could do no justice to you, God!
For the realization of oneness with
you and others eluded me.

Whatever acts I performed became offerings to God.
Whatever utterances I spoke became prayer.
Whatever the body consumed became oblations.
This is the way of the Parama Shiva.

—Lal Ded

All those possessions which are more than
what you need are worldly.
All the prayers offered and devoutness
observed by you
with an intention to
serve the self are worldly.

All actions in the fulfilment of one's
responsibilities
towards one's family
appear to be worldly—
however, they are not.

Have faith in God's will.
A dua (prayer) is only
to comfort the heart.
He gives us what is in our interest.

—Hazrat Nizamuddin

The natural attribute of the eyes is to see.
The eye enjoys the sight of beautiful things.
Eyes are meant to see the beautiful
and positive in this universe.
The nose has been created for a reason, to smell.
It loves sweet scents and fragrances and dislikes
bad smells and the stench of rotten things.
Similar, too, is the case of the ear.
The sounds that the ears can hear are of two kinds:
sweet sounds like the sound of the nightingale, and
displeasing ones like the crying of children.
Music is the sound with melody, rhythm, tune—
sweetness that may or may not have
meaning for the human being.
Through the practice of chanting, a
person's vibrations are transformed,
their chakras energized.
Chanting has the power to raise the mind, body
and spirit to a higher state of consciousness.

Prayer is a great necessity for the
development of the soul.
Prayer is a secret and a mystery that
people confide to God.

Even the angels in heaven pray for him who,
having performed his morning prayer,
remains sitting, engaged in the uninterrupted
meditation of God.

—Moinuddin Chishti

Ritualistic worship, yajna, and so on are nothing. Once one develops love for God, then one no longer needs these things. Until there is wind, one needs a fan; but when the southern breeze blows, one can put away the fan.

Unless you go to the physician, your disease will not be cured. It is not enough to be in the company of holy men once, their company is needed all the time; the disease is persistent. The other way is earnest prayer. He is your very own, tell Him, you want to see how He is—He has to come!

—Sri Ramakrishna

Never did help come from anywhere
but from yourself.
In your ignorance,
every prayer that you made
and that was answered,
you thought was answered
by some being;
but you answered the prayer
yourself unknowingly.

Each soul is potentially divine.
The goal is to manifest this divinity within
by controlling nature—external and internal.
Do this either by work, or worship,
or mental discipline, or philosophy—
by one, or more, or all of those—and be free.
This is the whole of religion.
Doctrines, or dogmas, or rituals, or books,
or temples, or forms are but secondary details.

—Swami Vivekananda

.12.

DISCOVER ONENESS

All I did was think about the body,
never once about what lies beyond.
I am no different from You—
never did this dawn on me!

—Lal Ded

Why is non-duality auspicious?
When the individual soul is of the nature of the
supremely real Self
nothing exists as non-separate as nothing is real.
Therefore non-duality alone is auspicious

An ignorant man differentiates between
the body, mind and intellect.
He does not know that he is a part
of the Supreme Being.

—Adi Shankara

When our hands and feet move, people say the body is moving! They do not know it is God who resides within who is moving. They say the hand got burnt in water! Water cannot burn anything. The hand got burnt by the heat that is in hot water. Rice is cooking in the pot. The vegetables are jumping inside. A child thinks the vegetables are dancing on their own! He doesn't know there is fire beneath! Similarly, human beings think the sense organs work on their own. They are not aware—it is pure consciousness that is within that makes things work.

I am asking you to give up the unripe 'I'—the 'I' that makes one attached to objects of desire. But I am not asking you to give up the mature 'I'...'I am God's servant, I am His child'—this is the mature 'I'.

—**Sri Ramakrishna**

The most important principle of
the environment is that
you are not the only element.

There is no difference between the soul of an
elephant and that of an ant.

—Mahavira

The Self is known to every one of us,
man, woman or child,
and even to animals.
Without knowing Him
we can neither live nor move,
nor have our being;
without knowing this Lord of all,
we cannot breathe or live a second.

—Swami Vivekananda

.13.

COMPASSION AND GENEROSITY

Do not ask for anything,
take what is given to you.

Keep what you need,
give the rest away to someone who needs it.
Wish for others only what you wish for yourself.
Do not approve of those deeds in yourself when you
disapprove of them in others.

—Hazrat Nizamuddin

Feelings of hatred and enmity are a curse.
For humanity to win, replace them
with mutual love and friendship.
If you wish to serve the Beloved (God),
you must serve others.
It is only in selfless service that
we see ourselves clearly.
The ego is smoothened and we learn humility,
tenderness, and love.

Among all the forms of worship, the one that
pleases the Almighty most is the grant of relief to
the humble and the oppressed.

—Moinuddin Chishti

If a householder practises charity without any
expectation of return, in the spirit of non-
attachment, he ends up doing good to himself.
It is not an act of 'helping' others.
It is service rendered to God who resides
in all beings.

Welfare of others—that is possible only for God—the
one who has created the sun and the moon, father
and mother, fruits and grains for the welfare of all
beings! The love that you see in parents is His love;
He has endowed them with love for the protection
of all beings. The compassion that you see in the
compassionate person, is His compassion, which He
has provided for the protection of the meek and
the helpless. Whether you show compassion or not,
He will work through some means or the other. His
work will not be disrupted.

—Sri Ramakrishna

Shed deceit, caprice, and untruth,
I tell myself.
Know that Shiva alone resides in one and all.
Why distinguish people then by their food,
drink, and customs?

—Lal Ded

When I think of my body, I am your servant.
When I think of myself as an individual,
I am a part of you.
But when I think of you and myself,
you and I are one.

—Adi Shankara

In happiness or sorrow, treat all creatures equally.
No living, sentient creature should be killed,
treated violently, abused, tormented or chased away.
Have compassion towards all living beings.
Hatred leads to destruction.
A person who is compassionate to
all living beings and whose love
embraces the whole universe
gets auspicious karmas.

—**Mahavira**

We are to worship the living
God, whom we see before us and
who is in everything we see.
We are to worship God
in all men and women,
in the young and the old,
in the sinner and the saint,
in the brahmin and the pariah,
especially the poor, the sick,
the ignorant, the destitute,
and the downtrodden.
For the God in them
wants our worship,
our care, and service.

I do not believe in a religion or God
which cannot wipe the widow's tears
or bring a piece of bread
to the orphan's mouth.

—Swami Vivekananda

Bring back those men who have gone astray,
enlighten those who live in delusion,
then all suffering shall be expelled from the world.
Make all living beings happy.

He who is loving and compassionate is able to give,
for he has banished hatred, envy, and anger.
The man of charity has found the path to Nirvana.
Like the man who plants a sapling to secure shade,
flowers, and fruit in the future
he finds joy in helping those in need.
That is the great liberation.

—The Buddha

.14.

THE SEARCH FOR THE TRUTH

What is knowledge and what is ignorance? So long
as you feel that God is far away, out
there somewhere, it is ignorance. When you feel
He is near at hand, it is knowledge.

Both knowledge and ignorance are states of the
mind. A human being is bound or free in the mind
itself, a saint or sinner in the mind. If a person can
practise continuous remembrance of God in the
mind, no other form of sadhana is required.

Not everybody can be a guru. Huge logs remain
afloat in water, and many birds and animals can
also cross the river aboard these. But if a creature
sits atop a log that is good for nothing, the log
sinks, taking with it the creature that is atop it.
That is why in every age, for the sake of guiding
humankind, God Himself takes human
birth as guru.

—Sri Ramakrishna

Intense desire is the desire to be liberated. True
knowledge is comprehension that the Self is true
and everything else is false.

Just as a light does not need another light to
illumine itself, similarly the Self needs no other
knowledge to make itself known, as the
Self is knowledge itself.

A man may bathe in the Ganga or in the sea,
he may be austere or give lavish gifts.
Yet all religions agree that none of
these will liberate him
if he does not acquire true knowledge.

The Supreme Being cannot be realized
by mere mastery over words.
A guru, and the rejection of all desire is
essential to find the Supreme Being.

The individual Self, heated in the fire of knowledge,
is free from all impurities and shines by itself like gold.
The ascetic with matted locks, the man
with shaven head,
The ascetic with his hair pulled out,
the man disguised in ochre robes,
they have eyes but do not see.
They disguise themselves to cheat the world.

—Adi Shankara

Knowledge comprises an unfathomable ocean.
Enlightenment is just a wave in that ocean.
While God alone sustains the ocean of knowledge,
enlightenment is the ambition of man.

Those having insight into the true 'essence of
things' are endowed with light like the sun.
They illuminate the whole world.

Crystal clear truth needs no praise.
If pursued with sincerity and humility, its brightness
showers special grace
and bliss on loving and compassionate souls.
Truth is complete only when accompanied by love,
compassion, mercy, and justice.

—**Moinuddin Chishti**

A master should only guide a
disciple's behaviour
through subtle hints.

With devotion and worship we come closer
to experiencing God's generosity.
It is at this stage that we need a guide.
He will break our illusions of perfection
and teach us the impermanence of reason.
His guidance will liberate you
and reveal the truth to you.

—**Hazrat Nizamuddin**

The mind is like
a furious elephant, but can be
controlled by the goad of
right knowledge.

Even limited knowledge of scriptures
is beneficial to a person
whose inner eye has opened,
just as the light of even one lamp
is enough to show the way
to a person whose eyes are open.

—**Mahavira**

When the inner light lit up within me,
off went the light outside.
In the darkness
I seized Him and held Him tight!

I enquired from my guru a thousand times:
what, after all, does nothingness mean?
He was quiet; I gave up and quietened too.
And it was from that silence, at last,
that no-thing emerged!

—Lal Ded

What is this universe? From what does it arise? Into
what does it go? In freedom it rises, in freedom it
rests, and into freedom it melts away. All human
life, all nature, is struggling to attain freedom.

—Swami Vivekananda

In no time this body will lie on the ground,
thrown away, unconscious, like a useless
log of wood.

Receive the good law of truth,
read it, understand it,
and preach it to all beings
in the universe.

—The Buddha

.15.

THE PATH

He who seeks must meditate upon freedom
in the shrine of his heart.
The intellect cannot understand it.
It is out of the reach of thought.
It is beyond the expression of speech.

People may quote the scriptures and
offer prayers to the gods;
they may perform rituals and worship deities.
But no liberation will be secured by these methods.
Only identification with the Supreme Being
will obtain liberation.

A man may bathe in the Ganga or in the sea,
he may be austere or give lavish gifts.
Yet all religions agree that none of these will
liberate him
if he does not acquire true knowledge.

—Adi Shankara

Another is the secret of worldly gain;
another is what proceeds to Nirvana.
Knowing it, a monk, the faithful follower of the
Buddha, without being elated at honours, shall
develop a liking for solitude.

This is the noble truth of the way that leads to the
cessation of pain:
this is the noble Eightfold Path.
That is, right views, right intention, right speech,
right action, right livelihood, right effort, right
mindfulness, right concentration.
The cause of pain is to be abandoned,
the cessation of pain is to be realized,
the noble Eightfold Path is to be practised.

—The Buddha

Meditation is the one thing.
Meditate!
The greatest thing is meditation.
It is the nearest approach
to spiritual life.
It is the one moment
in our daily life
that we are not at all material.

The road to good
is the roughest and steepest
in the universe.
It is a wonder that so many succeed,
no wonder that so many fall.
Character has to be established
through a thousand stumbles.

—Swami Vivekananda

Conquer your ego.
Pray to become selfless and
see the path illuminate before you.

Do not consider that being a master
or being a servant
is an obstacle in the way of God.
In this journey
there will be many hardships.
If you withstand
the ordeals of the world of love
you will be rewarded.

The path to achieving absolute renunciation
requires—not indulging in a profession
for sustenance; not asking for a loan;
concealing difficulties and not seeking any help
even if you have been starving for a week;
not saving for tomorrow; not praying to God
to wish harm on someone else.

—Hazrat Nizamuddin

God has made this world and blessed us with the
enchanting beauty of nature and the
human heart, both of which ought to
be admired and savoured.
So live before you die, because you
have been sent on this earth to live life
before you ultimately become one
with the Almighty.

Closest to Allah is one who possesses
the following three qualities:
magnanimity of a river, kindness of the
sun, and humility of the Earth.

—**Moinuddin Chishti**

Meditate in the depths of your mind, in a corner, and in the forest. And always discriminate between sat and asat*. God alone is sat—eternal, and everything else is asat—ephemeral. Discriminating thus, renounce the ephemeral in your mind.

Yearning! Just as a child cries helplessly for his mother when he cannot see her, if one cries for God with such yearning, one can even attain God by that.

—Sri Ramakrishna

---

*Non-existent, that is, subject to change and destruction, ephemeral, false.

What is the point of forsaking the home and heading to the forest? Why smear sacred ash and ointments on yourself? You are fine just the way you are! Bear God in your heart, that's all it takes!

Treading hundreds of paths to find God
the flesh of my feet wore out—in vain.
Then the One alone showed me the Only Way.
Oh how my story will tantalize all who hear it!

—Lal Ded

.16.

LIFE LESSONS

The Supreme Being is within all animals,
people and the gods themselves.
It is by the reflection of this Being that
the mind, body and senses are sentient.
But the Supreme Being within us is
concealed by the mind, senses, and body,
just as the sun is hidden by the clouds.
The person who, with perfect
understanding and wisdom,
always meditates on the Supreme
Being alone, he is my teacher.

Teacher: How do you see?
Student: I see with the help of sunlight.
Teacher: How do you see in the night?
Student: I see by the light of a lamp.
Teacher: How do you see the light? How do
you see even before you open your eyes?
Student: I see with my intellect.

Teacher: What helps you see that intellect?
Student: It is I.
Teacher: Then, you are that Supreme Light.
Student: I realize that I am.

—Adi Shankara

Self is an error, an illusion, a dream.
Open your eyes and wake up.
See things as they are.

One does evil.
One defiles oneself.
One avoids evil.
One purifies oneself.
Purity and impurity depend on oneself.
No one can purify another.

He who is awake will not be afraid of nightmares.
He who has recognized that the snake was
a rope ceases to fear.

—The Buddha

One who serves becomes the master.
Be the one to serve.
Only servitude will lead you to
being served in turn.

Do not consider that being a master
or being a servant
is an obstacle in the way of God.
In this journey
there will be many hardships.
If you withstand
the ordeals of the world of love
you will be rewarded.

If prosperity favours you,
spend that wealth
for the benefit of others. By doing so
you ensure that it never lessens.
If ever it was to slip out of your hands
do not have your eye on it.
It has no permanence.

—Hazrat Nizamuddin

Why thrash about in the dark like one blind?
If you are a Trika, just look within.
That is where Shiva resides, look no further.
Trust me. What I say is spontaneous and true.

Despite having eyes, be like the blind;
despite learning, like the fool.
Be deaf and mute though you can hear and
speak, and don't overthink.
Suspending all faculties, just be. Just be!

—Lal Ded

Non-violence and kindness towards living
beings is kindness to yourself.
For you are saved from sinning and
the consequent suffering.
Thus you can ensure your happiness.

We cannot achieve happiness if we make
another life unhappy, directly or indirectly,
intentionally or unintentionally.
That is the truth and we can experience this truth.

Live and let others live.
Don't hurt anyone.
Life is precious to all living beings.

That sacrifice is the greatest
in which austerity is the fire, the self the fireplace,
exertion the ladle, karma the fuel, and
self-restraint and tranquillity
the oblations.

—Mahavira

Live before you die.
Be present in every moment and
have deep gratitude for life.
The faithful do not die, they transcend
from this perishable world
to the world of eternal existence.

If you wish to serve the Beloved (God),
you must serve others.
It is only in selfless service that
we see ourselves clearly.
The ego is smoothened and we learn
humility, tenderness, and love.

The heart was essentially created for falling
in love with God and his creations.

—Moinuddin Chishti

It is all a matter of the mind. One is bound in the mind and free in the mind. The colour in which you dye your mind, the mind takes on that colour... It is all in the mind.... So, liberate your mind!

When the mind becomes free from attachment, one has the vision of God. Whatever comes into the pure mind, that is His voice. Pure mind, pure intelligence, pure atman—are all one and the same thing. There is nothing except God that is pure.

The kind of work that you are doing is good. If you can do it abjuring the idea that 'I am the doer' and without wanting to enjoy the fruits thereof, then it is very good. While working in such unattached manner, one develops devotion and love for God. One attains God doing work in such manner.

—Sri Ramakrishna

To preach the doctrine of shraddha
or genuine faith is the mission of my life.
This faith is one of the most potent
of factors of humanity.
First have faith in yourselves.
Know that though one may be
a little bubble and another
may be a mountain-high wave, yet
behind both the bubble and the wave
there is the infinite ocean.

The old religions said
that he was an atheist
who did not believe in God.
The new religion says that he is an atheist
who does not believe in himself.

—Swami Vivekananda

ACKNOWLEDGEMENTS

Grateful acknowledgement is made to the following copyright holders for permission to reprint copyrighted material in this book:

Aphorisms by Adi Shankara from 'You Are the Supreme Light': Life Lessons from Adi Shankara edited by Nanditha Krishna. Reprinted by the permission of the editor.

Aphorisms by the Buddha from 'See Things As They Are': Life Lessons from the Buddha edited by Nanditha Krishna. Reprinted by the permission of the editor.

Aphorisms by Mahavira from 'Live and Let Others Live': Life Lessons from Mahavira edited by Nanditha Krishna. Reprinted by the permission of the editor.

Aphorisms by Swami Vivekananda from 'Believe in Yourself': Life Lessons from Swami Vivekananda edited by Nanditha Krishna. Reprinted by the permission of the editor.

Aphorisms by Hazrat Nizamuddin from 'One Who Serves Becomes the Master': Life Lessons from Hazrat Nizamuddin edited by Bela Upadhyay. Reprinted by the permission of the editor.

Aphorisms by Lal Ded from 'Looking Within': Life Lessons from Lal Ded translated and edited by Shonaleeka Kaul. Reprinted by the permission of the translator and editor.

Aphorisms by Moinuddin Chishti from 'Be Present in Every Moment': Life Lessons from Moinuddin Chishti edited by Babli Parveen. Reprinted by the permission of the editor.

Aphorisms by Sri Ramakrishna from 'Liberate Your Mind': Life Lessons from Sri Ramakrishna edited by Arpita Mitra. Reprinted by the permission of the editor.

NOTES ON THE MASTERS

Mahavira (599–527/510 BCE) was a sixth-century reformer, philosopher, and the twenty-fourth Tirthankara of the Jains, credited with the establishment of Jainism as a distinct faith. An ardent believer in equality, he ordained men and women from all castes and classes and taught his disciples how to overcome the bondages of karma, liberate the soul, and practice sympathy, humility, non-attachment, and truthfulness. Born to a royal Kshatriya family near the ancient town of Vaishali, his parents were King Siddhartha of the Ikshvaku Dynasty and Queen Trishala of the Licchavi Republic. At the age of thirty, Mahavira left his worldly life to walk the path of spiritual awakening as an ascetic. After following an extremely austere lifestyle for twelve years, he accomplished kevala jnana in 557 BCE, a Jain concept that signifies omniscience or supreme wisdom. Mahavira preached five ethical principles that today form the bedrock of Jain thought: ahimsa (non-violence), satya (truthfulness), asteya (non-stealing), brahmacharya (chastity), and aparigraha (non-attachment).

According to the Svetambara tradition, Mahavira obtained nirvana in 527 BCE, while the Digambara tradition dates the event to 510 BCE. His teachings continue to guide millions in their pursuit of a way of life marked by compassion, moral integrity, and spiritual growth.

Buddha (563–483 BCE) was one of the greatest spiritual thinkers of the world. Born in present-day Nepal to King Suddhodana Tharu and Queen Maya of the Shakya clan, he lived an early life of great comfort until he stepped into the outside world and was deeply affected on observing the universality of suffering when he came across the 'four sights'—an aged man, a sick man, a dead man, and a religious ascetic. This profound experience persuaded him to renounce his worldly life rooted in the comforts of the palace and search for deliverance from old age, illness, and death. At the age of thirty-five, after many years of living as an ascetic, he attained enlightenment in

Bodh Gaya and became the Buddha. As a teacher, the Buddha sought a middle path between eternalism and annihilationism. The Four Truths of Buddhism—life is suffering, craving causes suffering, the end of suffering can be brought about the end of craving, and there is a path away from craving and suffering—gives rise to the concept of the Eightfold Path which guides an individual on how to live life without attachment and with the right intentions. Together, the Four Truths and the Eightfold Path are the basis of Buddhist teaching and are followed by people all across the globe who practice its core values such as meditative practices, righteousness, kindness, and mindfulness.

According to religious sources, the Buddha died at the age of eighty, near Kushinagara, having achieved mahanirvana, a state of absolute spiritual release.

Adi Shankara (eighth century CE) was one of the greatest theologians of India and the most celebrated exponent of the Advaita Vedanta philosophy that advocates for a singular reality and all other differences being illusory. Possibly born in the first half of the eighth century CE in modern Kerala, he studied and mastered complex ancient scriptures under his guru,

Govinda Bhagavatpada. Adi Shankara wrote invaluable commentaries on the Brahmasutra, the ten principal Upanishads, and the Bhagavad Gita and played a crucial role in solidifying modern Hinduism by unifying multiple sects and engaging in discourse with scholars from different schools of philosophy to restore the authority and relevance of the Vedas. His original works contain innumerable gems of thought on establishing oneness with the Supreme Being, equality and caste, self-realization, knowledge, pride, attachment, and moksha. He has composed several poems, praising Hindu deities. Known as 'stotras', the ones dedicated to Krishna and Shiva are considered to be the most significant.

Adi Sankara travelled across the length and breadth of the country—from Kanyakumari in the south to Kashmir in the north and Dwarka in the west to Puri in the east—to propagate his philosophies and establish several monasteries inspired by ancient hermitages. These centres have ensured the continuity of his teachings in the modern world.

Moinuddin Chishti (1136–1235), also known as Gharib Nawaz or the benefactor of the poor, was a venerated saint known for strengthening the Chishti order of Sufism in India. Born in Sistan in present-day southeastern Iran, he arrived in South Asia in the early thirteenth century and settled in Rajasthan, where he attracted a substantial Hindu and Muslim following. Moinuddin Chishti was the first Islamic mystic in India who encouraged the use of music as 'sama' along with prayers and meditation to establish an intimate and personal connection with God. His life was marked by a dedication to spreading the message of love, peace, humility, and tolerance. In his sermons, Chishti preached about renouncing materialism, searching for God within oneself, and caring for all fellow creatures, irrespective of their religion and status. His key teachings speak of charity and compassion for the poor and helpless, leading an untainted life of devotion to the Divine, and achieving oneness with God in the service of his creations.

After he died in 1235, Moinuddin Chishti's tomb in Ajmer, the Dargah Sharif, became a place of pilgrimage for thousands of devotees from across faiths for centuries, thereby emerging as a symbol of religious harmony and coexistence.

Hazrat Nizamuddin (1238–1325) was a prominent Sufi mystic of the Chishti Nizami order during the thirteenth and fourteenth centuries whose teachings left an indelible mark on the spiritual and cultural landscape of the subcontinent. Born into a poor Sayyid family in Badaun, Uttar Pradesh, he inherited the spiritual legacy of Fariduddin Ganjshankar, Qutbuddin Bakhtiyar Kaki, and Moinuddin Chishti. He lived in Delhi before building his khanqah in Ghiyaspur, a place that attracted people from all walks of life. Hazrat Nizamuddin's teachings were deeply rooted in the Sufi tradition of compassion, sympathy for the oppressed, and complete trust in the Divine. He believed in the idea of universal love and equality, emphasizing that the path to God is open to all, regardless of their backgrounds. His teachings encouraged people to shun superficial distinctions based on socio-economic status and connect with the divine essence within themselves and others. His most famous disciples included the renowned poet and musician Amir Khusro, Nasiruddin Chiragh Dehlavi, Akhi Siraj Aainae Hind, and Burhanuddin Gharib. His life was marked by a disregard for religious orthodoxy and political hegemony.

He died on 3 April 1325. Hazrat Nizamuddin's dargah is located in Delhi. Centuries later, his teachings continue to inspire his devotees who flock to his dargah in search of solace.

Lal Ded (1320–92) was a Kashmiri poetess, saint, and mystic of the Shaivism persuasion. Locally known as Lalleshwari, much of her biographical history is part of the indigenous oral traditions of the region. Believed to be born into a Brahmin family near Srinagar, it is said that she left an unhappy marriage and became a follower of Siddha Srikantha, also known as Siddhamol, a Shaivite spiritual master. She travelled long distances on foot, collecting alms for survival, narrating her own proverbs and quatrain-based poetry, and finally emerging as a revered teacher. Lal Ded's immense contribution to Kashmiri literature is her characteristic style of poetry called vaakh, today considered a symbol of her revolt against the gatekeepers of knowledge. Through the vaakhs, she beautifully articulated her profound thoughts on a diverse range of subjects such as life, dharma, woes of the human condition, and the realization of God as pure consciousness in the language of the common people—a decision that made spirituality accessible to people irrespective of their caste, creed, gender, and socio-economic position. Her poetry is a soulful marriage of Sanskritic, Islamic, Sufi, and Sikh cultures and has been translated and performed across the world.

Although there is no confirmation through historical accounts, a grave near Bijbehara is attributed to Lal Ded.

Sri Ramakrishna (1836–86) was a revered Indian mystic whose teachings were centred on the understanding that the Ultimate Reality of life is one, and it is indicated by different names in different religions. He was born Gadhadhar Chattopadhyay, in the village of Kamarpukur, sixty miles northwest of Calcutta, to Kshudiram Chattopadhyaya and Chandramani Devi. As the child of poor but pious parents, Sri Ramakrishna experienced an episode of ecstasy when he was only six years old while watching white cranes flying against black clouds. He would continue to experience such intense spiritual moods throughout his lifetime. In 1855, when the Kali Temple at Dakshineshwar was consecrated, he became its first chief priest under the patronage of Rani Rasmani. Sri Ramakrishna ardently upheld the harmony of religions. He professed that while each religion has its nuances and differences, they are valid as long as every path leads to the realization of God through devotion. His philosophies formed a significant bridge between modernity and spirituality, stressing on the importance of prayer, truthfulness, and selfless service, while rejecting greed, pompous religious practices, and miracle-mongering.

Sri Ramakrishna died of throat cancer in 1886, surrounded by his devoted disciples and his consort, Sri Sarada Devi. In his final days, he laid the foundation for a monastic brotherhood which was then taken forward by his foremost student, Swami Vivekananda. Today the organization is known as Ramakrishna Math.

Swami Vivekananda (1863–1902) was a nineteenth-century philosopher, nationalist, and monk credited with introducing Vedanta philosophy, modern Hindu thought, and Yoga to the Western world in the Parliament of World's Religions in Chicago in 1893. Born as Narendranath Datta into an influential Bengali family in Calcutta, Swami Vivekananda found himself drawn to spirituality and religion from an early age, captivated by Hindu scriptures, gods and goddesses, and wandering ascetics. In November 1881, he met Sri Ramakrishna—a turning point in his life—who would show him the path to realize God through renunciation, prayer, and selfless service of one's fellow men. In his teacher's final days, Swami Vivekananda and several other disciples received ochre robes, and he was asked to lead the monastic brotherhood known as the Ramakrishna Math. In 1881, he began extensively travelling around India, engaging with people from all walks of life and studying diverse religious traditions to develop a deeper understanding of suffering and poverty so he could find ways to uplift the country. In 1893, he made a tremendous impact in Chicago where he appeared as a spokesperson for Hinduism, before going on to travel across the United States of America, the United Kingdom, and British Ceylon to speak about Vedanta, Yoga, and Hindu spiritualism.

On 4 July 1902, he died while meditating in the monastery at Belur Math, his pupils believing that he attained mahasamadhi.